Relax, You're Going to Die

Snow Falling in Moonlight: Odes in Praise of Dogen's Shobogenzo / *Twelve Poems based on Dogen's Shobogenzo:The Treasury of the True Dharma Eye*

Warm Zen Practice: A Poetic Version of Dogen's Bendowa / *Whole Hearted Way*

Collections / Spiritual

Buddha's Golden Light: *Collected Works of Tai Sheridan*

Patanjali: Yoga Sutras in Lingo: *The Liberation of Spirit in Modern Metaphors*

Relax, You're Going to Die

by Tai Sheridan, Ph.D.

Table of Contents

Introduction

If you scratch beneath the surface, you will find that many of your anxieties, worries, and fears are associated with death and dying. *Relax, You Are Going To Die* is an invitation to examine your relationship with death and your ability to live with grace and dynamic vitality.

If we examine death, we usually ask: What happens when I die? What happens after death? Where did I come from? Will I be reborn? What role does God or a deity play in life and death? What is the meaning of living and dying?

Buddhists ask a different question. They ask: Who is doing the asking?! This question results in an examination of the ego, which is your accumulated personal and conditioned identification. When you lessen the hold that your ego has on the full experience of your body, heart, and mind, perhaps, you may glimpse your life as an integral part of the fabric of all of existence. The death of the ego is the birth of true living.

The question of death and dying is an inseparable part of a spinning two headed coin. One side says "dying", and the other says "living". I wrote the poetic contemplations in this book in order to help you see the spinning coin more clearly and to help you deepen your relationship to the mystery of living and dying, which is the basis of living a wise, kind, and beneficial life.

Dedication

To the Great Mystery

He not busy being born is busy dying.

Bob Dylan

Death is the Root

Death is the root
of your core anxiety

Relaxation is the root
of your core aliveness

Until you make
peace with death
it is impossible to relax
in the core of yourself

Until you relax
in the core of yourself
it is impossible to
make peace with death

Your intellect can't resolve
this chicken egg existential paradox
yet without resolution
you will succumb
to angst dread loneliness grief
for not claiming your
birthright of contentment

Understanding living and dying
is the core of a deeply
rooted spiritual life

Dying is Ongoing

Dying is an
ongoing event

With every breath
you are dying
With every breath
you are living

Living and dying
are present each
moment of your life

Being vitally alive
is a function of
your awareness about
how you live
and how you die
each moment

Breathing and awareness
are the gates to the garden
of living and dying

Being close to your breath
transforms spiritual philosophy
into spiritual experience

Death Isn't Abstract

Death isn't
an abstract event

Making it abstract intellectual
a belief or other worldly
protects you from deep grief

To make peace with death
you need to make
peace with grief

It requires tremendous
inner strength to dwell deeply
inside the loss of those
you dearly love

It requires
the same strength
to dwell deeply
inside the knowledge
that you will lose
your precious life

You may tend to avoid
accepting the biggest truth
about living which is
that everything dies

Deep acceptance will
change you forever

Free Falling into Dying

When you are afraid
of death you contract
and thoughts muscles emotions
become tense narrow hardened

Fear of death is death itself

You become desperate for
a soft cushion to land on
to protect you from facing
what you know will arrive

There is no soft cushion
there is only free falling into dying
that is now that is forever
it can't be stopped or started
because living dying
being loving
is life itself

To Die Before You Die

To die before you die
is the secret of the spiritually awake

What dies is your self-centered ego
and personal identification
with the stories that you have told yourself
for as long as you can remember
about who and what you are
as a separate person

which you have reinforced
to substantiate yourself

and which
the world has reinforced
to substantiate you

you sadly have come to believe
that the fiction you call me
is the whole story

our impoverished ego
only knows how to protect itself
from the mysterious truth that
there is no substantiality whatsoever
to hang on to and call me

this is strange
wondrous magical
hard to understand
hard to accept
hard to realize

but if you are committed
to making peace with death
then your journey will take you
to understanding that
who you call me is a dream

'Me' Dying

When you think of 'me' dying
it disconnects you from
the fabric of your existence

Which is the intimate bond
you have with everything that is alive
and with everything that has or will exist
how could you possibly be separate
from any single thing

The fact is that
if everything that exists
throughout all time space
didn't exist as it is was will be
then you wouldn't be here

The miracle is that your body
is made of atoms and minerals
formed in interstellar space
the miracle is that who you are
can never be separated from
the totality of all existence

Death is the door to radically changing
your perspective on what is going on
in the depths of your Being

Death's Door

You can't think about death's door
without thinking about birth's door

These are the two doors of your life
the one you came in
and the one you will go out

Which is a half truth
because although your body
was conceived by a man/woman
womb grown and worldly born
and although your body will decompose
ashes to ashes dust to dust

It doesn't account for the fact that
you are part of a huge cosmic event
that defines you as bigger
than just the distance
between these two doors

Fear of Death

The fear of death is the fear of total aliveness
which isn't excitement or fulfilling dreams

At the core of dynamic living
is a great presence not just of yourself
but of the whole works of existence
as it courses through your veins
and pumps oxygenated moonlight
through synapse and cell

It is the certainty
that you exist
connected to everything
your feet on the ground
your breath flowing freely
your eyes wide open
celebrating the joyful
shimmering of things

In this great presence
life and death soften into
the warm embrace of whatever
you call holy sacred divine
blissful true real

Relax You're Going to Die

If you want full aliveness
which is presence and deep peace
which is acceptance of your living and dying
within the very big cosmic living and dying

Then take a fresh spring breath
and exhale whatever you are holding on to
in your body emotions mind spirit
and die into this precise moment

Fighting death is fighting life
if you have ever been trout fishing
you know that a fish on a hook won't relax
how could he know about catch and release
which is what the universe is
always doing with your life

There is only one mantra
one string of sacred words
that makes any sense
which will relieve you
of the sleepless nights
locked jaws addictive habits
anxious days depressed emotions
beating yourself up

Living as if your life
isn't the heartbeat of god
the breath of buddha
the prayer of allah
the blood of christ
the embodiment
of everything
you call holy

In still waters golden light
may you imbibe the gentle truth
Relax, you're going to die

You Are Death

Everything comes and everything goes
this is the law of reality

Gathering atoms turn into shapes
you give it a name like cup or body
it lasts a second an eon thirteen billion years
then it parts like a wave from the shore

a strange voice in your head
tells you to aim at some ideal state
strong true kind perfect creative loving
which is stupidity that will drive you mad
and keep you from inner peace

You can't achieve any state that lasts
especially relaxation so the best you can
do is return again and again
to that which will sustain and regenerate
presence vitality love generosity
breathing living dying

Which allows you living to the max
being yourself and nobody else
then you are ready to die
a thousand deaths each day
and celebrate the joyful stream
while mourning autumn leaves
and winter's chill

You are life you are death
you are you and you are cosmos
in this knowing you can stop
calling it yourself calling it by any name
in the silence of your inner heart
the mystery magic of living dying being

Your destiny is to sit in the theater
watching the movie that you
will never completely understand
which makes it a sacred blessing
for which you can offer up your thanks
and the whole of your life

Death the Great Leveler

The desert fathers gave up everything
to live in a cell in the hot desert
the benedictines chant vespers
while the rest of us are sleeping
zen monks walk through morning shadows
without a trace of themselves

Rumi Hafiz Kabir
lost in ecstatic poetry
Whitman pounded the ground
with the cacophony
of body love humanity

You have longed for truths heard
why keep them distant
why put your peace in another's hands

Give up everything
which doesn't mean sell it or go broke
just stop your death grip
on people places things
stop claiming things as yours
it's just another way of avoiding
death the great leveler

Death is an invitation to simplicity
simplicity is an invitation to clarity
clarity is an invitation to relaxation
relaxation is an invitation to presence
presence is an invitation to living
living is an invitation to death

Death is an Invitation

The only way to learn relaxation
is to learn how and when
you tense up forget the why

Catch yourself stumbling into
tight shoulders clenched fists
sucked in belly gnarled forehead

Headaches heartaches backaches
bone aches muscles aches
so many things make you want to shout
I can't stand it anymore

In this tension is your death
which is an invitation to relaxation
which is your life
which is your rebirth
from now to now
from frozenness to suppleness
from rigidity to softness
from you to everything
from ego to buddha

From a complicated confused existence
to a simple alive flowing life

Philosophy of Death

If you want to relax
in the dream of living dying
consider your philosophy
because it keeps you
stuck insane or free happy

Your fear of death
keeps you from being truly alive
so why not embrace dying
your fear of life
keeps you from jumping in
with both feet and experiencing
the infinite array of your own potential
so why not make room
for the totality of you

Scrambling after wealth fame love
all the goodies you think
will make you happy
is a death sentence

Why not grab the key
hanging in your brain heart
on a tree moon in a child's face

Bathe in the fresh night breeze
breathe out until there's nothing left
allow the gap to close between
your living and your dying
until you are set free to roam
green mountains walk city streets
sit still in a rocker as the lights dim
in the magic of being

Dying into Redwoods

I often lean against a redwood tree
and die into the bark
my spine rising
into the blue of sky

My legs become roots
journeying down
into unseen waters
my breath slows softens
my eyes open in wonder
great cumulous clouds
dance over the mountain peak

Soon I'll return
to kids computers stress and modern plagues
but for this moment I choose
to let what I conveniently call myself die
and I dwell in the house of relaxation and peace
where you and I are inextricably entwined
in the living and dying of all things

A Wish for the World

May All Beings Be Happy!

May All Beings Be One!

May All Beings Be Free!

About the Author

Tai Sheridan is a poet, philosopher, and Zen priest. He transforms ancient Buddhist and Zen texts into accessible and inspirational verses. His *Buddha in Blue Jeans* series offers a contemporary approach to Buddhist philosophy and awakening.

Made in the USA
Middletown, DE
03 July 2020